Our Country, Our Flag

Patricia Almada

Contents

Rigby

A Harcourt Achieve Imprint

www.Rigby.com
1-800-531-5015

Hello, my name is Ms. Cruz.
This is our country's flag.
It is red, white, and blue.

Let's ask some questions to learn more about our flag.

How. many
stars and stripes
are on the flag?

Our flag
has 50 stars
and 13 stripes.

Yes, now I see.
I wonder what the next
question will be.

Has our flag changed?

Our first flag had only 13 stars, one for each state. Now our flag has 50 stars for 50 states.

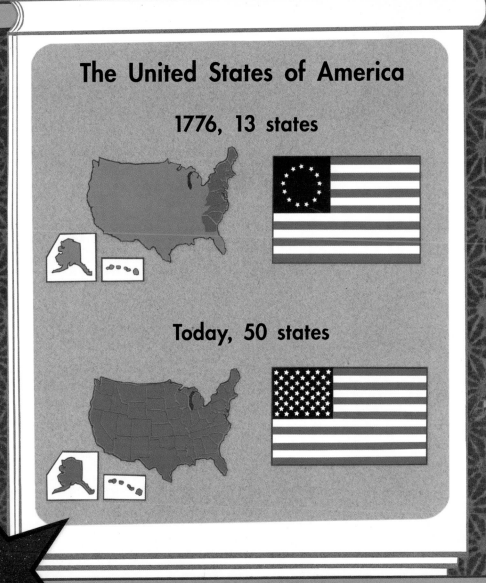

The United States of America

1776, 13 states

Today, 50 states

Yes, now I see.
I wonder what the next
question will be.

Why do we fly
our flag?

People fly the flag
to show love
and respect
for our country.

8

Yes, now I see.
I wonder what the next
question will be.

What do we call
our flag?

Our flag has
many names.

I call it "Old Glory."

We call it "the Stars and Stripes."

Yes, now I see.
I wonder what the next
question will be.

11

Where can I see the flag?

You can see the flag at school, around town, and even at the zoo!

Yes, now I see.
I wonder what the next
question will be.

Who owns the flag?

The flag belongs to everyone in the U.S.A.

Yes, now I see.
This is **our** flag.
It belongs to you and me!

Glossary

Flag

Star

Stripes

**United States
of America**